Houghton
Mifflin
Harcourt

SCIENCESAURUS®

A STUDENT HANDBOOK

Photo credits start on page 153.

Printed in the U.S.A.

ISBN 978-0-544-07958-8 (hardcover)

12   0868   21 20 19 18 17

ISBN 978-0-544-08030-0 (softcover)

15 16 17 18   0928   21 20 19 18

4500703106   A B C D E F G

Table of Contents

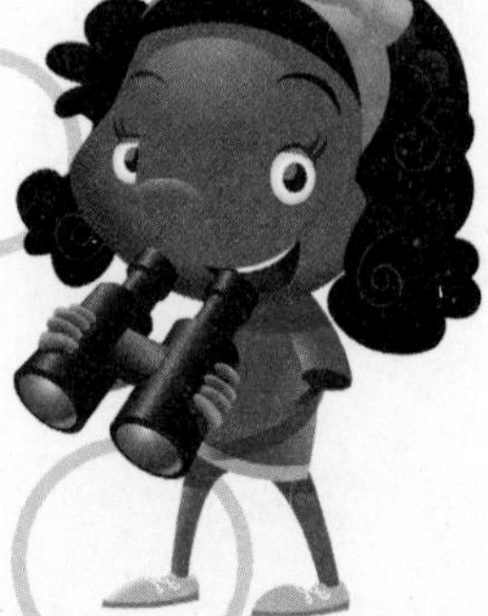

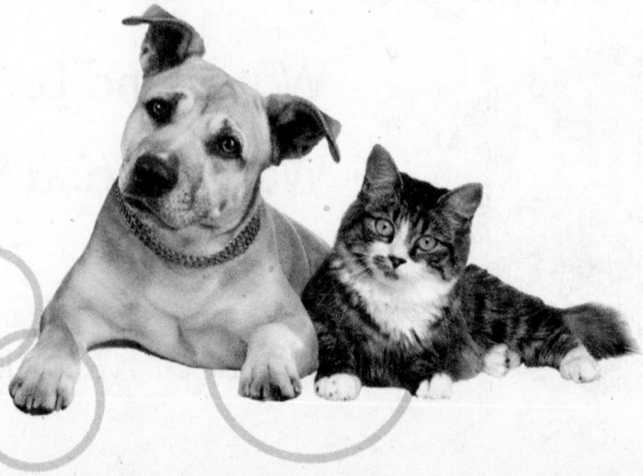

How to Use This Book

Here are three ways to find information in *ScienceSaurus*.

1. Look in the Table of Contents.

Look for big subjects, such as *plant* or *space*. The Table of Contents begins on page iii.

2. Look in the Index.

Look for smaller subjects, such as *bird* or *sun*. The Index begins on page 149.

3. Look in the Glossary.

Look for a science word to find its meaning. The Glossary begins on page 129.

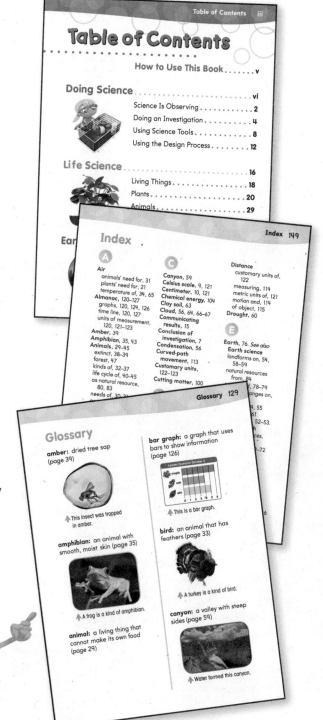

Doing Science

What kind of dog makes the best scientist?

Have you ever wondered why? Why is the sky blue? Why do animals have fur? Why does water freeze into ice? These are questions answered by science. **Science** is the study of the natural world. A person who studies science is a **scientist**.

Science Is Observing

You can be a scientist. Start by observing the world around you. To **observe** means to use your five senses to help you learn. You use a different body part for each sense.

sight

hearing

smell

taste

touch

See Also

Observing Properties
Page 93

Science Alert!
Observing uses more than just your sense of sight. It uses the other four senses, too.

Your Five Senses

Different senses help you learn different things.

▲ Your sense of **sight** helps you learn how things look.

▲ Your sense of **touch** helps you learn how things feel.

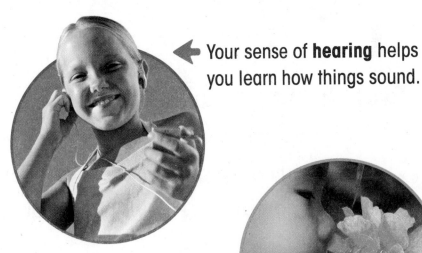

◄ Your sense of **hearing** helps you learn how things sound.

◄ Your sense of **taste** helps you learn which foods you like.

▲ Your sense of **smell** helps you learn how things smell.

Doing an Investigation

Observations lead to questions. Scientists try to answer questions by doing investigations. An **investigation** is a way to find out the answer to a question.

Steps for an Investigation

An investigation often has these steps.

Step 1: **Ask a question.**

Suppose you make an observation about your guinea pig. She seems to like some plants better than others. So you ask a question.

What plants does my guinea pig like best?

Step 2: Make a hypothesis.

You have to change your question so you can test your idea. To do this, you need a hypothesis. A **hypothesis** is an idea that tells what will happen. It can be tested. You can state a hypothesis.

My guinea pig will choose lettuce more often than carrots.

Step 3: Plan a test.

Now you have to find out if your hypothesis is true. So you plan a test. A **test** is a way to observe and measure what happens.

First, I give my guinea pig lettuce and carrots at feeding time.

Then, I observe which one my guinea pig chooses first.

Last, I do this for two weeks.

Step 4: Gather materials.

Make a list of your materials. Then gather them.

MY LIST

- ☑ lettuce
- ☑ carrots
- ☑ paper
- ☑ pencil
- ☑ guinea pig

Step 5: Follow your plan.

Do your investigation.

I follow my plan.

Step 6: Record your data.

Write down what you observe. A table is a good way to keep track of the data.

Date	Lettuce	Carrots
May 3	✔	
May 4		✔
May 5		✔
May 6		✔
May 7		✔
May 8	✔	
May 9		✔

What My Guinea Pig Chooses First

Step 7: Draw conclusions.

Look at your data. Is there a pattern? Is this what you thought would happen? You can draw a conclusion. A **conclusion** explains a pattern that you see in the data.

My investigation shows that my hypothesis is not correct. I can now draw a conclusion.

Step 8: Communicate your results.

You can share the results of your investigation. You may write a report or make a poster. Then others can learn from what you did.

My conclusion is that my guinea pig likes carrots better than lettuce.

Carrots or Lettuce?

My guinea pig likes carrots better than lettuce.

Using Science Tools

Scientists measure as they collect data. They use many kinds of tools.

Hand Lens

A **hand lens** makes things look larger than they are. Here is how to use one.

1. Hold the hand lens close to your face.

2. Move the object until you see it clearly.

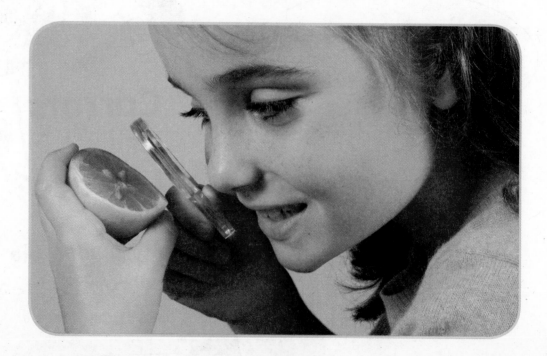

Thermometer

A **thermometer** measures temperature. Temperature is measured in units called **degrees**. Here is how to use a thermometer.

1. Place the thermometer where you want to measure temperature.

2. Wait two minutes.

3. Find the top of the liquid in the thermometer. Find the mark on the thermometer next to it.

4. Read the number by the mark. That is the temperature.

The temperature is 70°F.

Did You Know?
The United States uses the **Fahrenheit scale** to measure temperature. Many other countries use the **Celsius scale**.

See Also

Temperature
Page 65

Units of Measure
Pages 121–123

Ruler

A **ruler** is a tool that helps you measure how long something is. Use a yardstick or a tape measure to measure longer distances. Here is how to use a ruler.

1. Put the edge of the ruler at the end of the object.

2. Read the number at the other end.

This leaf is 6 inches long.

See Also
Units of Measure
Pages 121–123

Did You Know?
The United States uses inches, feet, and yards to measure length. Many other countries use centimeters and meters.

Measuring Cup

A **measuring cup** is a tool that helps you measure how much liquid there is. Here is how to use it.

1. Pour the liquid into the cup.

2. Put the cup on a table.

3. Wait until the liquid is still.

4. Look at the level of the liquid.

5. Read how much liquid is in the cup.

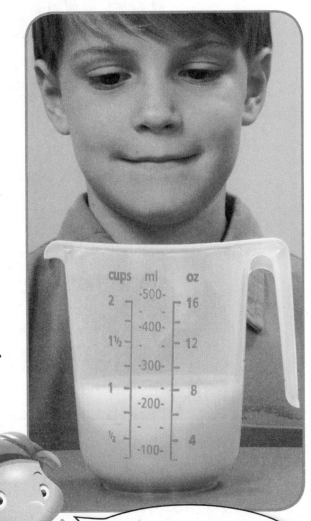

There are 8 ounces of liquid here.

Did You Know?
The United States uses ounces, cups, and gallons to measure liquids. Many other countries use milliliters and liters.

See Also

Units of Measure
Pages 121–123

Using the Design Process

Engineers solve problems by using math and science. They try to solve problems by using a design process. A **design process** is a set of steps that engineers follow to solve problems.

The Design Process

The design process has these steps.

Step 1: Find a problem.

Suppose you have trouble finding your drawing supplies. So you name your problem. You need to find a way to store your drawing supplies. You brainstorm ways to solve the problem.

I need an organizer for my stuff!

Step 2: Plan and build.

You choose a solution to try. You make a plan. You draw and label your plan. You choose the best materials to use.

pencils

can

paper

tape

I use the materials to follow my plan.

Pencils
Markers
Crayons

Step 3: Test and improve.

You test your organizer to see whether it works.
Does it solve the problem?

The organizer works for tall pencils.
The shorter markers and crayons
are hard to reach.

Step 4: Redesign.

You think of a way to make
your organizer better.

I added cans that are different
heights. Now I can get to the
shorter markers and crayons.

Step 5: Communicate.

You write and draw to show what happened.
You can share what you learned with others.

Life Science

How do you like my garden?

Look at the garden. Can you find plants, animals, and people? They are all living things.

How can you find out about living things? You can study life science. **Life science** is the study of living things.

I think it's growing on me!

Living Things

Plants, animals, and people are living things. **Living things** need food, water, and air to grow and change. Living things can **reproduce**, or make other living things like themselves.

Rocks, water, and bridges are nonliving things. **Nonliving things** do not need food, water, and air. They cannot reproduce.

nonliving things

living things

Living or Nonliving?

You can tell if something is living or nonliving. This chart shows how.

Living or Nonliving?			
What is it?	Does it need food, water, and air?	Does it grow and change?	Can it reproduce?
	yes	yes	yes
	no	no	no
	no	no	no
	yes	yes	yes

You can tell that the living things are the duckling and the flower. The nonliving things are the toy and the rock.

Plants

Many kinds of plants grow on Earth. Grass and trees are plants. Shrubs and bushes are plants, too. Some plants are so small you can hardly see them. Others are as tall as towers.

All plants are alike in some ways. Every **plant** is a living thing that uses sunlight to make food. A plant grows in one place. It cannot move from place to place on its own.

See Also

Plants
Page 81

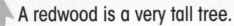 A redwood is a very tall tree.

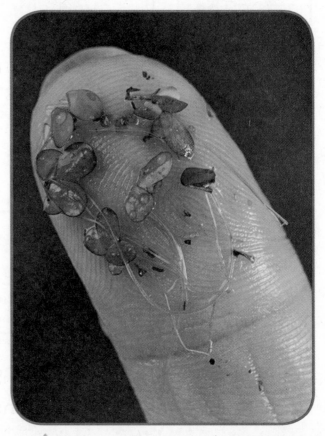

⬆ Duckweed is a very small plant.

What Plants Need

Plants need air, light, and soil to live.

Air and Light

A plant's leaves use air and sunlight to make the plant's food. The food gives the plant energy to grow.

▲ Plants need air and light.

Water

A plant needs water to grow and stay healthy. Water helps the plant make food. It also moves food to all the parts of the plant.

▲ Plants need water.

Soil and Nutrients

Most plants live in soil. Soil has **nutrients**, or materials that help a plant grow. Soil also helps hold the plant in place.

▲ Plants need nutrients from soil.

The Right Amounts

Different plants need different amounts of sunlight and water. A plant needs the amount of sunlight and water that is right for it. If a plant gets too much or too little of any one thing, it may die.

Each plant needs the right kind of soil. Many plants grow well in soil with a lot of nutrients. Some plants can grow in sandy soil. Other plants do not need soil at all. They need just nutrients, water, and air.

This cactus needs a lot of sunlight, but little water.

This flower needs a lot of water, but little sunlight.

This flower does not need soil. It gets nutrients from material on tree bark.

Parts of a Plant

Plants have different parts. Most plants have roots, stems, and leaves. Many plants also have flowers, fruits, and seeds.

Each plant part helps the plant get what it needs. Then the plant can live and grow.

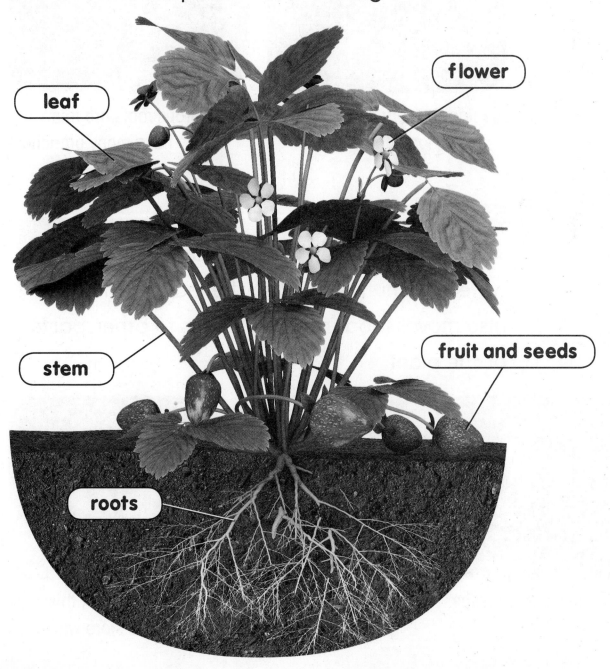

leaf

flower

stem

fruit and seeds

roots

Roots

The **roots** take in water and nutrients from the soil. They also hold the plant in the soil.

⬆ Taproots are thick. They store food and water.

⬆ Fibrous roots are thin. They have many branches.

Stems

The **stem** helps hold up the plant. It moves water and nutrients up to the leaves. The stem also moves food from the leaves to other parts of the plant.

⬆ Stems hold up tulips.

⬆ Bushes and trees have woody stems.

⬆ The stems of this cactus store water.

Leaves

The **leaves** use sunlight, air, water, and nutrients to make food for the plant.

fern

aspen

spruce

maple

aloe

Leaves from different plants are different shapes and sizes.

Flowers, Fruits, Seeds

The **flowers** help the plant reproduce, or make new plants. Flowers make fruits. The **fruits** hold seeds. A **seed** is the part of a plant from which a new plant grows.

flower

fruit

seeds

⬆ This zucchini flower has made a fruit.

⬆ The fruit of the apple holds seeds.

Science Alert!
Not all plants have flowers. Some plants use cones to make seeds.

cone

How Plants Grow

Most plants grow from seeds. Most seeds have a covering called a seed coat. The **seed coat** protects the seed. The seed has stored food and the beginning of a young plant. The young plant uses the stored food when it begins to grow.

When a seed gets water and warmth, it may **germinate**, or start to grow. This is the beginning of the plant's life cycle. A **life cycle** is made up of all the changes a living things goes through during its life.

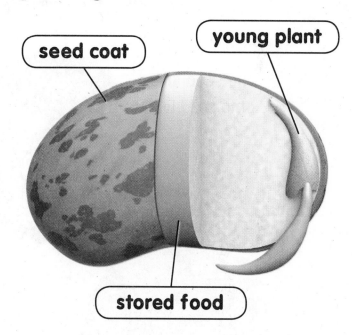

seed coat

young plant

stored food

Did You Know?
Not all plants grow from seeds. A fern does not grow from a seed.

fern

The Life Cycle of a Flowering Plant

The life cycle of a plant with flowers starts with a seed. The seed grows to look like the parent plant. The adult plant makes new seeds. Then the cycle begins again.

The Life Cycle of a Bean Plant

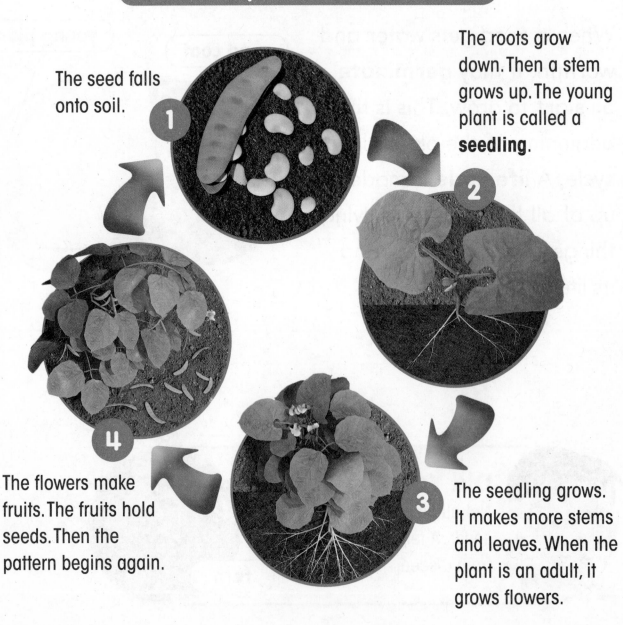

The seed falls onto soil.

1

The roots grow down. Then a stem grows up. The young plant is called a **seedling**.

2

The seedling grows. It makes more stems and leaves. When the plant is an adult, it grows flowers.

3

The flowers make fruits. The fruits hold seeds. Then the pattern begins again.

4

Animals

Think about animals you know. Some have fur. Others have feathers or scales. Some animals have bones. Others do not.

All animals are alike in some ways. Every **animal** is a living thing that cannot make its own food. An animal eats plants or other animals. Most animals move from place to place on their own.

How are these animals alike and different?

What Animals Need

Animals need food, water, air, and space to live.

Food

Different animals eat different kinds of food. Some animals eat only plants. Some eat other animals. Some animals eat both plants and animals.

⬆ A koala eats leaves.

Water

An animal needs water to grow and stay healthy. Some animals drink water. Other animals also get water from the food they eat.

⬆ Zebras drink water.

See Also

Animals
Page 83

Water
Pages 86–87

Science Alert!
Camels can go a long time without water. The fat in their hump can be used for water and energy.

Air

Animals need air to live. Special body parts help them get air. Some animals have lungs. Others, like fish, use **gills** to breathe in water.

▲ This bison's mouth and nose take air into its lungs.

Space

Every animal needs space to live and have its young. Some animals find or build homes. Others find shelter when they need it. Shelters help animals keep safe. They also help some animals surprise and catch other animals.

gills

▲ A shark uses gills to breathe.

▲ A weaver bird makes a nest that looks like a basket.

▲ This eel lives in holes in rock and coral.

Different Kinds of Animals

Scientists group animals by how their body parts are alike.

Mammals

A **mammal** is an animal that has hair or fur. The hair or fur keeps the animal warm and protects its skin. Mammals use lungs to breathe. **Lungs** are body parts that take in air.

A mother mammal makes milk and feeds it to her young. Most young mammals are born live.

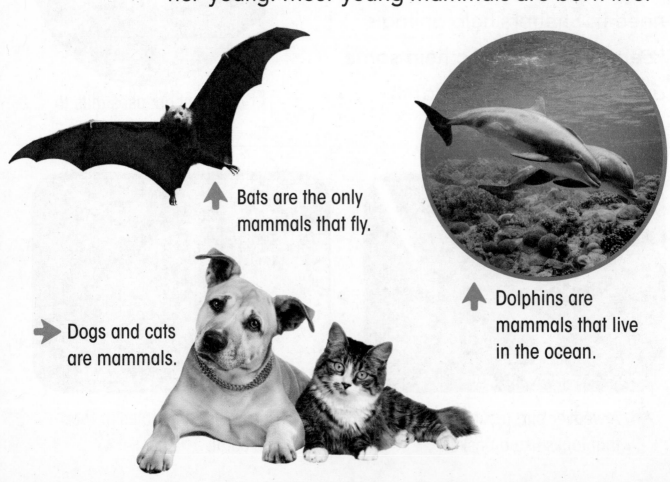

▲ Bats are the only mammals that fly.

▲ Dolphins are mammals that live in the ocean.

➡ Dogs and cats are mammals.

Birds

A **bird** is an animal that has feathers. The feathers keep a bird warm and help it fly.

A bird has two wings, two feet, and a beak. Most birds use their wings to fly. Birds use lungs to breathe, as mammals do.

A mother bird lays eggs. Young birds hatch from the eggs.

← Ducks are birds that can fly and swim.

▶ Turkeys are birds.

▲ Parakeets are birds that can be kept as pets

Science Alert!
Not all birds can fly. Penguins can't fly, but they can swim.

Reptiles

A **reptile** is an animal with rough, dry skin covered with scales. Its skin protects it. Reptiles use lungs to breathe, as mammals and birds do.

A reptile's body does not always stay at the same temperature. It changes with the air temperature.

Most mother reptiles lay eggs. Often they do not care for their young after the eggs hatch.

Alligators warm themselves in the sun.

Snakes do not have legs at all.

Sea turtles have flippers instead of legs.

Amphibians

An **amphibian** is an animal with smooth, moist skin. Its skin helps it live both in water and on land.

A mother amphibian lays eggs in water. Most young amphibians hatch and grow in water. They use tails to swim and gills to breathe.

Young amphibians change as they grow into adults. Adults have legs and most live on land. They use lungs to breathe.

← Frogs and toads live in places where their skin can stay damp.

Did You Know?
If a salamander loses a leg, it will grow a new one.

Fish

A **fish** is an animal that lives in water and breathes with gills.

Most fish are covered with scales. The scales protect the fish. They also help the fish move easily in water. Most fish have fins, too. They use fins to swim.

Most mother fish lays eggs. Young fish hatch from the eggs. Other fish are born live.

Sailfish live in salt water. They may travel many miles looking for food.

Trout live in lakes and other bodies of fresh water.

Parrot fish live on coral reefs in warm salt water.

Insects

An **insect** is an animal that has three body parts and six legs. Many insects also have wings and can fly.

An insect does not have bones. It has a hard covering on the outside of its body. This covering protects the soft body parts inside.

Most insect mothers lays eggs. Some insects lay hundreds of eggs at one time.

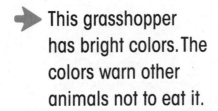
This grasshopper has bright colors. The colors warn other animals not to eat it.

Bees sting to keep themselves or their hives safe.

The walking stick has a body that looks like a twig.

Science Alert!
Spiders are not insects. Spiders have eight legs, not six.

Extinct Animals

Dinosaurs and other kinds of animals lived long ago. But they are no longer living today. These animals are extinct. **Extinct** means that no members of a kind of living thing are still alive.

Scientists know about extinct animals by studying fossils. A **fossil** is what is left of an animal that lived long ago.

People can see fossils at museums.

Scientists find many kinds of fossils in rock.

Some fossils are bones, teeth, and shells that have turned to rock.

Some fossils are prints of body parts made in mud. The body part rots away, but its shape stays in the mud. Slowly the mud turns to rock.

Scientists find fossils in tar and amber. **Amber** is a tree sap. An animal gets trapped in tar or amber and dies. Over time, it becomes a fossil.

⬆ This insect was trapped in amber.

⬆ A scientists digs out a dinosaur bone that has turned to rock.

⬆ A fish left a fossil in the rock.

Animal Life Cycles

All the changes that an animal goes through from birth to death make up its **life cycle**. Each animal group has its own kind of life cycle.

Life Cycle of Mammals

A young mammal starts growing inside its mother's body. When it is big enough, it is born.

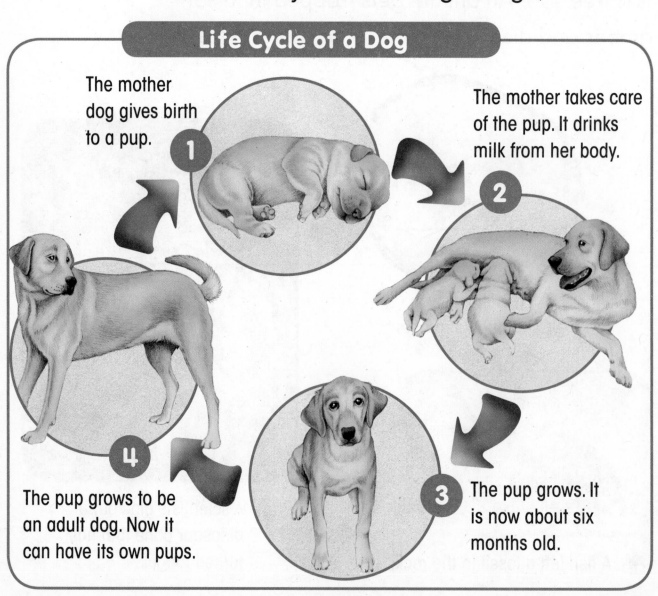

Life Cycle of a Dog

The mother dog gives birth to a pup. **1**

The mother takes care of the pup. It drinks milk from her body. **2**

3 The pup grows. It is now about six months old.

4 The pup grows to be an adult dog. Now it can have its own pups.

Life Cycle of Birds

A mother bird lays eggs. A chick grows inside each egg. When it is too big for the egg, the chick hatches.

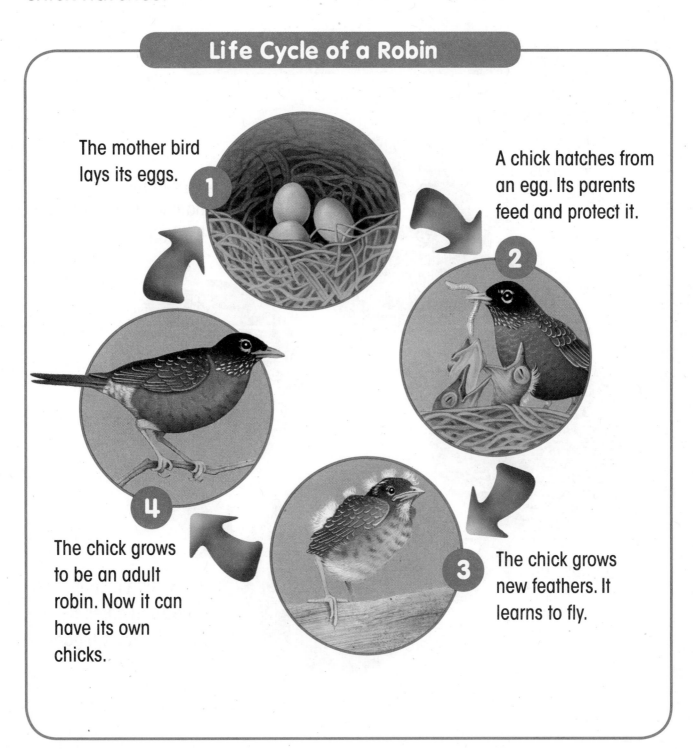

Life Cycle of a Robin

The mother bird lays its eggs.

1

A chick hatches from an egg. Its parents feed and protect it.

2

4

The chick grows to be an adult robin. Now it can have its own chicks.

3

The chick grows new feathers. It learns to fly.

Life Cycle of Reptiles

Most young reptiles start growing inside eggs. When a young reptile gets too big for an egg, it hatches. It looks like its parents.

Life Cycle of a Python

The mother python lays eggs. She keeps them warm.

1

A young python hatches from its egg. Its mother leaves.

2

When the python is an adult, it can reproduce.

4

The young python feeds and cares for itself. It grows bigger.

3

Life Cycle of Amphibians

A mother amphibian usually lays its eggs in water. When a young amphibian hatches, it does not look at all like its parents. As it grows, it changes many times.

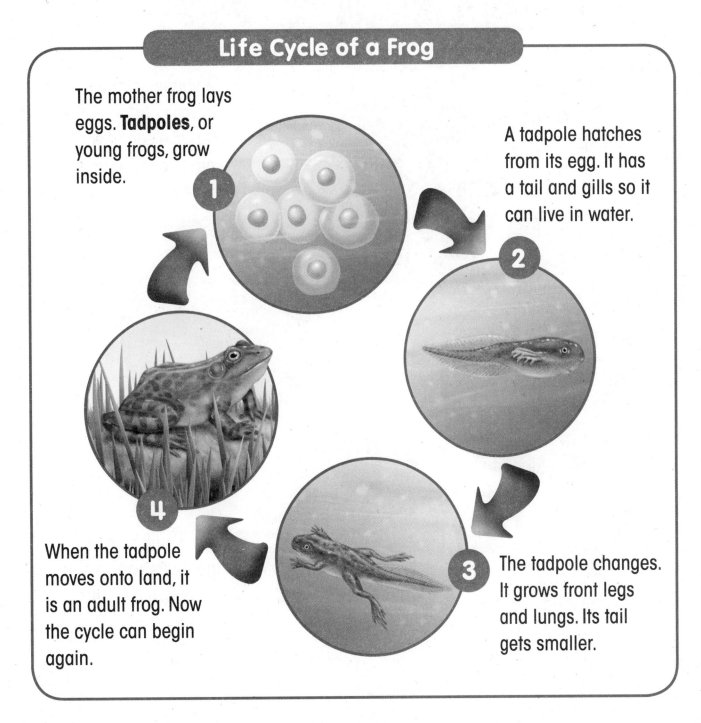

Life Cycle of a Frog

The mother frog lays eggs. **Tadpoles**, or young frogs, grow inside.

1

A tadpole hatches from its egg. It has a tail and gills so it can live in water.

2

The tadpole changes. It grows front legs and lungs. Its tail gets smaller.

3

When the tadpole moves onto land, it is an adult frog. Now the cycle can begin again.

4

Life Cycle of Fish

Most mother fish lay eggs. Young fish grow inside. When the eggs hatch, the young fish do not look like their parents.

Life Cycle of a Salmon

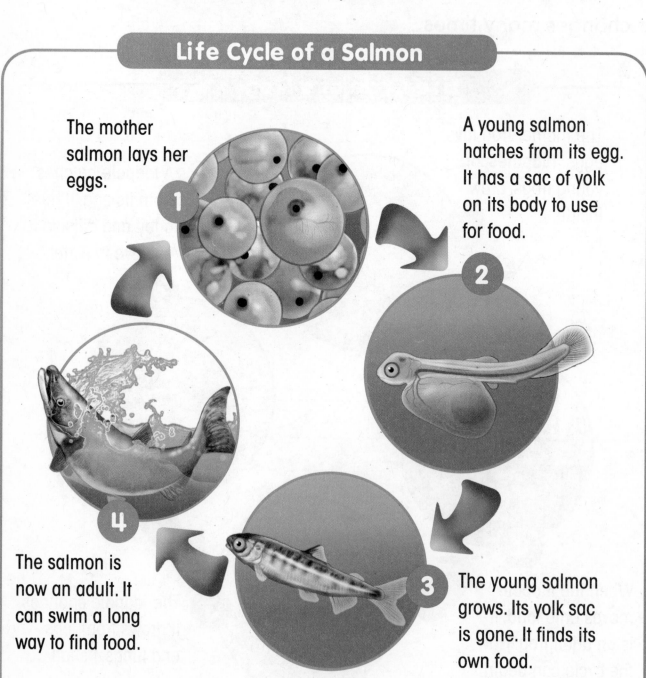

The mother salmon lays her eggs.

1

A young salmon hatches from its egg. It has a sac of yolk on its body to use for food.

2

3

The young salmon grows. Its yolk sac is gone. It finds its own food.

4

The salmon is now an adult. It can swim a long way to find food.

Life Cycle of Insects

Most mother insects lay eggs. When a young insect hatches, it does not look at all like its parents. As the insect grows, it changes many times.

Life Cycle of a Butterfly

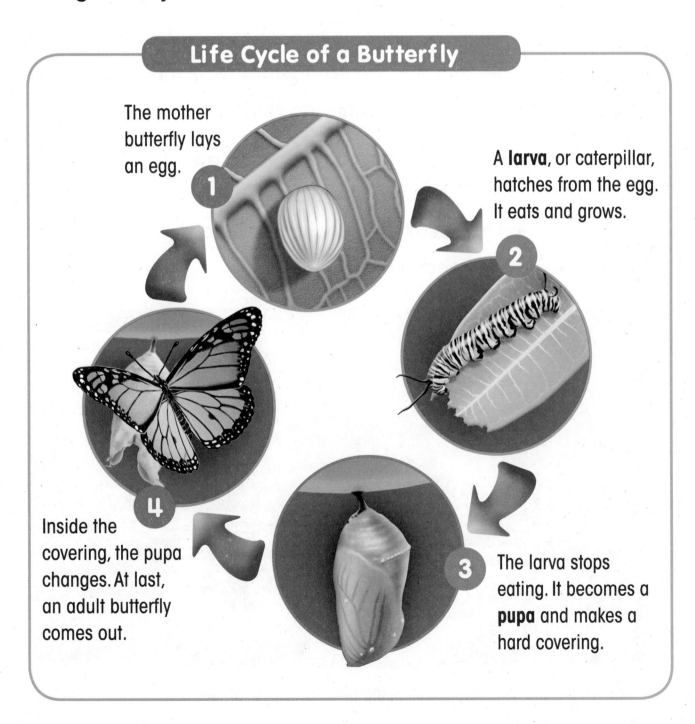

The mother butterfly lays an egg.

1

A **larva**, or caterpillar, hatches from the egg. It eats and grows.

2

3 The larva stops eating. It becomes a **pupa** and makes a hard covering.

4 Inside the covering, the pupa changes. At last, an adult butterfly comes out.

Environments and Ecosystems

Plants and animals find what they need in their environment. An **environment** is made up of all the living and nonliving things in a place.

An **ecosystem** is all the living and nonliving things found in one place. Living things can live only in ecosystems where they can get what they need.

See Also

Natural Resources
Page 80

nonliving things

living things

 This pond ecosystem has living and nonliving things.

Forests

One kind of ecosystem is a forest. A **forest** is a place that gets enough rain and warmth for many trees to grow.

Some trees grow tall in a forest. Their leaves catch the sunlight they need to make food. Bushes and other plants need less sunlight. They can grow below the trees. Forest animals use trees and plants for food and shelter.

When the weather turns cold, many trees in a forest lose their leaves. Food is hard to find. Some birds fly to warmer places. Other animals sleep all winter.

See Also
Forests
Page 82

woodpecker

bear

raccoon

Deserts

A **desert** is an ecosystem that gets very little rain and lots of sunlight. Only a few kinds of plants and animals can live there. Desert plants and animals do not need much water.

Most desert plants store water to use when they need it. Some plants have thick leaves with a waxy coat. Others hold water in their stems.

Desert animals have ways to stay cool and get water. Some animals stay in the shade and look for food at night when it is cooler. Other animals get water from their food.

Not all deserts are hot. Any place that gets less than 10 inches of rain a year is a desert.

hawk

dove

elf owl

burrowing owl

hare

gila monster

Grasslands

A **grassland** is an ecosystem that is mostly dry. It gets only enough rain for grasses and wild flowers to grow. Few trees and shrubs can live there.

When the weather turns cold, the grasses cannot grow. Their deep, dense roots keep them alive until it gets warm again.

In a grassland, large animals eat the grasses. Smaller animals find food and shelter among the grasses or in the soil.

bison

prairie chickens

prairie dogs

monarch butterfly

Rain Forests

A **rain forest** is an ecosystem where rain falls almost every day. Most rain forests are also warm all year round. Rain and warm weather help many trees and plants grow.

Rain forest plants grow at different levels. Trees may grow very tall to get sunlight. Little light reaches down below the treetops. Only plants that do not need much light can live there.

Many animals live in the rain forest because they can find food easily. Different animals live at different levels. Many birds live near the treetops where they can find fruit to eat. Other animals find food and shelter among the tree leaves.

morpho

sloth

toucan

anaconda

jaguar

Oceans

An **ocean** is a very large, deep body of salt water. Plant-like algae live near the ocean's surface. Algae are food for some fish and other ocean animals.

Ocean animals find what they need in ocean waters. Many swim to places where they can find food. Other animals live in shallow water where sunlight can reach the ocean floor. These animals eat other tiny animals or algae that grow there.

See Also

Water on Earth
Page 55

Water
Pages 86–87

herring

dolphin

starfish

lobster

Earth Science

Look up in the sky. Look out at the ocean. Look at the land all around you. Sky, water, and land make up Earth.

How can you find out about Earth? You can study Earth science. **Earth science** is the study of planet Earth and objects in the sky.

What does the ocean say to the shore?

Nothing. It just waves!

Water and Land

Earth is made up of water and land.

Water covers most of Earth. All living things need water to stay healthy. Many plants and animals live in water, too.

Land covers the rest of Earth. Many kinds of living things live on land.

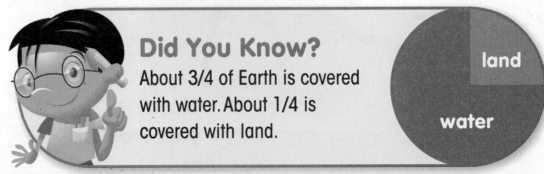

Did You Know?
About 3/4 of Earth is covered with water. About 1/4 is covered with land.

Water on Earth

Water on Earth may be salty or fresh. A large body of salt water is called an **ocean**. Most water on Earth is in oceans. The rest of the water on Earth is fresh water. Fresh water is not salty.

You can find fresh water in most streams, rivers, and lakes. A **stream** is a small body of flowing water. Some streams flow into rivers. A **river** is a large body of flowing water. A **lake** is a body of water with land all around it.

ocean

stream

river

lake

Only 1 drop of every 100 drops of water on Earth can be used by people. The rest is salty, which people can't use.

See Also

Oceans
Page 51

Water
Pages 86–87

The Water Cycle

Water on Earth moves from Earth's surface into the air and back again. This movement of water between Earth and the air is called the **water cycle**. The water cycle takes place over and over again.

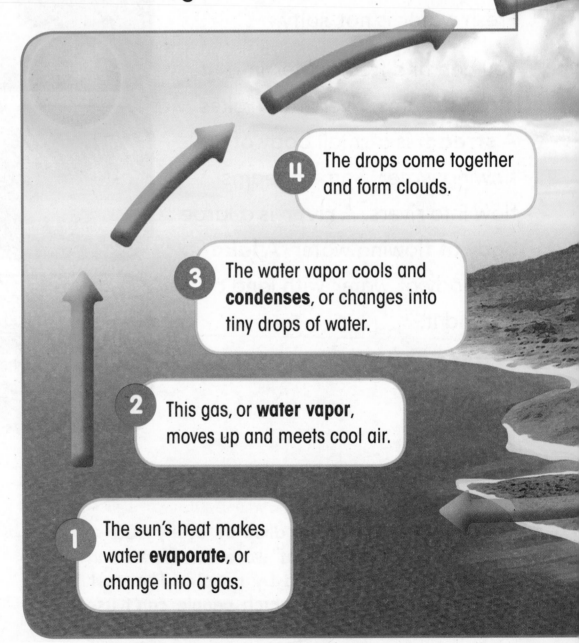

4 The drops come together and form clouds.

3 The water vapor cools and **condenses**, or changes into tiny drops of water.

2 This gas, or **water vapor**, moves up and meets cool air.

1 The sun's heat makes water **evaporate**, or change into a gas.

See Also

Water Can Change
Pages 102–103

5 The water drops become bigger and heavier. Then they fall as precipitation. **Precipitation** is rain, snow, sleet, or hail.

6 The precipitation flows into streams and rivers. Rivers flow into lakes and oceans. Then the water cycle begins again.

Landforms

A **landform** is a natural land shape on Earth's surface. Earth has many kinds of landforms.

High Landforms

Mountains are landforms that are much higher than the surrounding land. Landforms that are rounded and much smaller than mountains are **hills**.

mountains

hills

Did You Know?
Some islands are the tops of undersea mountains.

Low Landforms

A **valley** is the low land between mountains or hills. The sides of valleys are not usually steep. A valley with steep sides is called a **canyon**.

valley

canyon

Flat Landforms

A **plain** is a flat land that spreads out over a long distance. A **plateau** is a flat land that is higher than the land around it. It is high like a mountain, but flat on top.

plain

plateau

The Changing Earth

Earth is always changing.

Slow Changes

Some changes are slow. They may take months or many, many years. Weathering, erosion, and drought are slow changes.

Weathering happens when wind and water break down rock into small pieces.

Erosion happens when wind and water move rocks and soil. This changes the shape of the land.

A **drought** is a long time with very little rain. Without rain, the land gets very dry. The soil may blow away.

⬆ Weathering and erosion formed this arch.

⬆ Erosion washed away the land near this beach.

⬆ In a drought, plants cannot grow.

Fast Changes

Some changes are fast. They may happen in just minutes, hours, or days. Earthquakes, volcanic eruptions, and floods are fast changes.

An **earthquake** is a shaking of Earth's surface.

A **volcano** is a mountain with an opening in Earth. When a volcano erupts, hot melted rock comes out.

A **flood** happens when streams, rivers, or lakes overflow onto land. The water washes away soil to new places.

⬆ An earthquake made this road fall away.

⬆ This volcano in Hawaii erupts often.

⬆ Floods may cause a lot of damage.

Word Watch!

The word *volcano* comes from the name *Vulcan*. Vulcan was the old Roman god of fire.

Rocks

Rocks are hard, nonliving objects from the ground. Different rocks have different properties. A **property** is one part of what something is like.

Rocks may be different colors, shapes, or sizes. Rocks may be rough or smooth. They may be hard or soft.

See Also

Observing Properties
Page 93

obsidian

granite

sandstone

pumice

lapis

Did You Know?
Sand is made up of tiny grains of rock.

 Soil

Soil is the loose top layer of Earth's surface. It is made up of small pieces of rock and bits of once-living things.

Soil forms when wind and water break down rock. The bits of rock form the base of the soil. At the same time, dead plants and animals fall to the ground. These once-living things break down into small pieces. Those pieces mix with the bits of broken rock.

Soils have different properties. Different soils may be made up of different kinds of rocks. Some soils have more once-living things than other soils.

Types of Soil

▲ **Clay** soil has very tiny rock bits.

▲ **Loam** has a lot of plant and animal bits.

▲ **Sandy** soil has bits of rock you can see.

Weather and Seasons

Look out the window. Is it sunny, cloudy, or rainy? Is it hot or cold? **Weather** is what the air is like outside.

sunny   cloudy   rainy   snowy

The weather changes from day to day and from month to month. The changes in weather follow the same pattern each year. The patterns follow the seasons. A **season** is a time of year that has a certain kind of weather.

Temperature

An important part of weather is temperature. **Temperature** is a measure of how hot or cold something is. It is measured with a tool called a **thermometer**.

The temperature of the air changes during the day. In the daytime, the sun warms the air. The temperature goes up. At night, the sun does not warm the air. The temperature goes down. The air feels cooler. Air temperature also changes from day to day and from season to season.

See Also

Thermometer
Page 9

Temperature
Page 123

The air usually warms up in daytime.

The air usually cools down at night.

Clouds and Precipitation

Clouds are made of many tiny drops of water. The drops may join and get heavier. When the drops get too heavy, the water falls to Earth as **precipitation**. Some kinds of precipitation are rain, snow, sleet, and hail.

Rain

The temperature of the air affects the kind of precipitation that falls. If the air is warm, rain falls. **Rain** is water that falls from clouds.

rain

Did You Know?
Fog is a cloud that touches the ground.

Snow

If the air is very cold, the water in the air freezes. It falls to Earth as snow. **Snow** is solid water that falls from clouds.

snow

Sleet

When rain falls through freezing air, the raindrops turn to ice. These small lumps of ice are called **sleet**.

sleet

Hail

Pieces of ice that fall from clouds are called **hail**. The pieces may be as small as tiny peas or as big as grapefruits. Hail often forms in very cold rain clouds during summer thunderstorms.

hail

Hail is ice, but it usually falls in the summer.

Wind

Wind is moving air.

One way to measure wind is by its direction. Wind can blow from the north, south, east, or west, or any point in between.

Wind is also measured by its speed. Sometimes the wind blows gently. Sometimes it blows very hard. Wind that blows too hard can knock down trees or break up buildings.

| no wind | light wind | medium wind | strong wind |

You can look at a flag to tell how hard the wind is blowing.

Spring

The four seasons are spring, summer, fall, and winter. Each season has a weather pattern.

Spring is the season that follows winter. The air gets warmer. There are more hours of daylight in spring. In many places, rain falls often.

spring

Warmer air and more rain help plants start to grow. Many farmers plant seeds in spring. In spring, many animals have their young. The growing plants are food for some young animals.

In many places, tulips bloom in spring.

Summer

The season that follows spring is **summer**. It is the warmest time of year. The days are often hot and sunny. Summer storms may make the weather change quickly.

summer

Summer's heat and sunlight help plants grow flowers and fruits. In summer, young animals eat and grow. Some begin to look like adults.

Many children are not in school in summer.

Did You Know?
In the U.S., the longest day of summer is in June. South of the equator, the longest day of summer is in December.

 Fall

Fall is the season that follows summer. The air gets cooler. There are fewer hours of daylight in fall.

fall

With the cool air and less sunlight, some plants make seeds. Fruits and vegetables are ready to be picked. Then some plants die. The leaves of some trees change color and then drop off.

When plants stop growing, animals have less food. Some animals store food for winter. Some animals move to other places.

In fall, you may need to wear a sweater when you go outside.

Winter

Winter is the season that follows fall. Winter is the coldest time of year. In many places, the air is cold enough for snow. Many trees have bare branches.

winter

People wear heavy coats when it snows in winter.

In other places, winter is only a little cooler than other seasons. These places may never have snow. Many trees stay green, and crops still grow.

Space

Look up at the sky. During the day, you may see the sun. At night, you may see stars and the moon. The sun, stars, and moon are all objects in space. **Space** is the area in all directions beyond Earth.

There are too many stars in the sky to count them all.

Observing the Sky

The day sky looks different from the night sky.

The Day Sky

The largest and brightest object in the day sky is the sun. The **sun** is the closest star to Earth.

The sun is made of hot gases. The gases give off light and heat. The sun's light makes the sky bright in the daytime. The sun's heat warms Earth's land, air, and water.

⬆ The sun gives light and warmth to Earth.

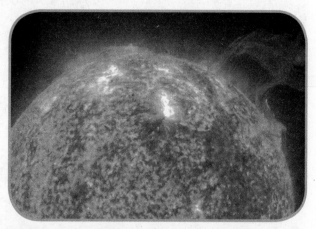

⬆ This close-up photo of the sun was taken with a special camera.

Be Careful!
Never look directly at the sun. It can hurt your eyes.

The Night Sky

On a clear night you can see many stars. A **star** is a big ball of hot gases. The hot gases give off light. This light is what you see from Earth. Stars look tiny because they are far away.

On many nights, you can see the moon. The **moon** is a huge ball of rock that circles Earth. It seems to shine, but the moon does not give off its own light. Light from the moon comes from the sun.

Stars may be white, blue, yellow, orange, or red.

People have visited the moon. This shows the first visit in 1969.

Science Alert!

The moon does not change shape. It just appears to. During any month, you may see shapes like these.

Planets Around the Sun

On some nights you may see Mars and Venus in the sky. Mars and Venus are planets. Earth is a planet, too. A **planet** is a large ball of rock or gas that moves around the sun. A planet's path is called its **orbit**.

Eight planets move around the sun. Together the sun and planets make up the **solar system**.

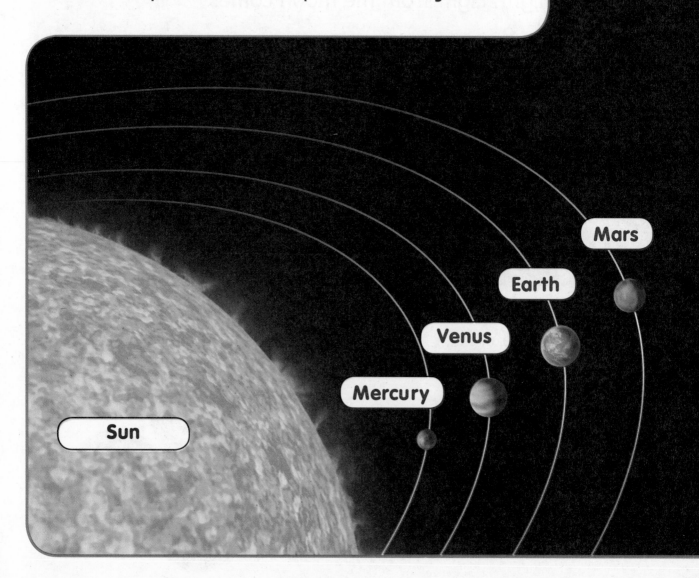

Sun

Mercury

Venus

Earth

Mars

Neptune

Uranus

Saturn

Jupiter

The objects in this picture are not the right size or distance apart. Because the sun is so big, a model with the right sizes and distances would make some of the planets too small to see.

Day and Night

Each day the sun seems to move across the sky. But the sun does not really move at all. It is Earth that is moving. Because Earth moves, we have day and night.

Earth rotates, or spins, around and around like a top. This spinning is called **rotation**. It takes about 24 hours for Earth to rotate one time. One full rotation is one full day.

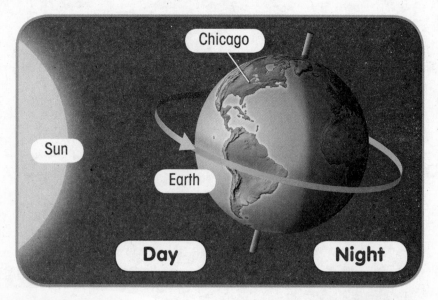

This is Chicago during the day.

Earth's rotation causes each part of Earth to have light and dark each day. When one side of Earth faces the sun, that side is lighted. It is daytime. When that side of Earth faces away from the sun, that side is dark. It is nighttime.

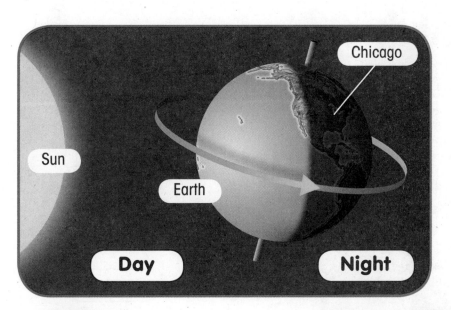

Natural Resources

See Also

Environments and Ecosystems
Page 46

People need air, water, food, and shelter. They get these things by using natural resources. A **natural resource** is anything found in nature that people can use.

plants

animals

soil

water

rocks

Some important natural resources are plants and animals. Rocks, soil, and water are natural resources, too.

Plants

Plants are natural resources. They can be used to make many products people need.

People use plants for food. They eat fruits and other plant parts. People also use plants to make foods such as bread and pasta.

Cloth can be made from plants. People use the cotton plant to make cloth for clothes and many other products.

See Also

Plants
Page 20

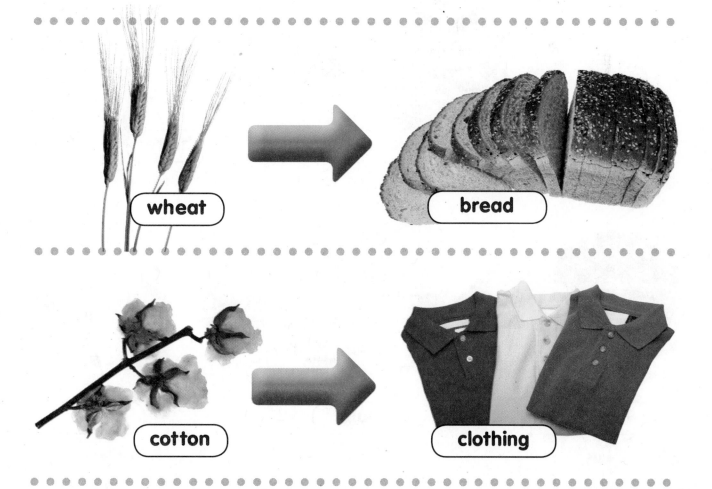

wheat → bread

cotton → clothing

Forests

People use trees from forests for many things. People use wood to build furniture and houses. They may burn wood for fuel.

People also use wood to make paper. Chips of wood are used to make a mix called pulp. The pulp is pressed flat to make sheets of paper.

See Also

Forests
Page 47

wood → chairs

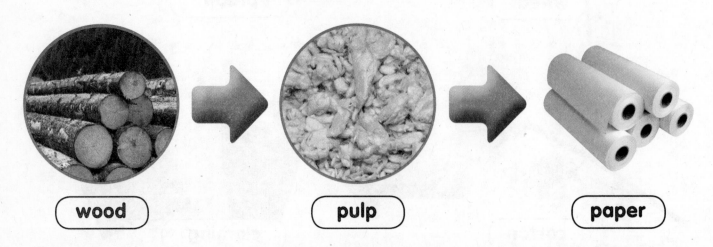

wood → pulp → paper

Animals

Animals are natural resources.

Animals and animal products are food for people. People eat meat, eggs, and fish. They drink milk and use it to make cheese, yogurt, and other dairy products. Honey is another animal product people eat.

See Also

What Animals Need
Page 30

People use animal products to make clothing. Wool from sheep and goats is used to make sweaters and coats. Silk from silkworms is made into clothing, too. Leather from animal skins is made into shoes and belts.

clothing

eggs

honey

milk

shoes

Resources from Earth

Some natural resources are dug out of the ground. They have many uses.

People use rocks to build buildings and roads. Marble is a rock that people carve into statues. People melt sand to make glass.

Iron and copper are also found in the ground. First, they are melted down. Then, they can be used to make things. Copper is used to make wire and pots. Iron is mixed with other materials to make steel. Steel is used to make bridges, tools, and many other things.

See Also

Rocks
Page 62

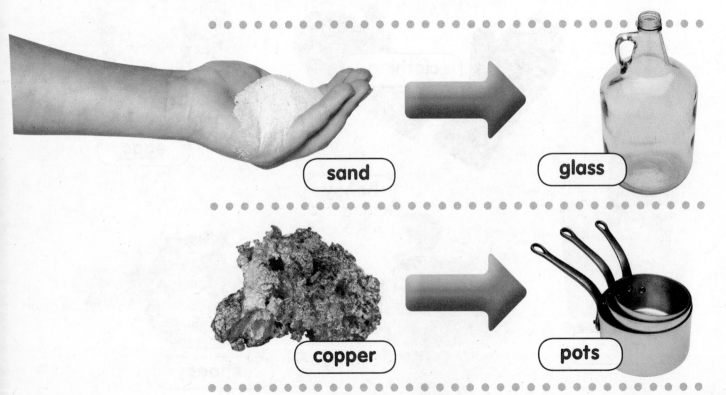

sand

glass

copper

pots

Land and Soil

People need land. They build houses and other buildings on some land. People use other land for yards and parks.

Soil is an important natural resource. Farmers use soil for growing crops and raising animals. Without soil, most plants could not grow. Then animals would not have food.

People use some soils to make useful goods. Bricks, pottery, dishes, and tile are made from soil.

See Also

What Plants Need
Pages 21–22

Soil
Page 63

Most living things on land depend on soil.

Water

Water is a natural resource that all people, animals, and plants need to live.

People use fresh water every day for drinking, cooking, and bathing. They also use water for washing clothes, dishes, and many other things.

Animals and plants need fresh water, too. Wild animals and plants get fresh water in their environments. On farms and in homes, people give animals and plants the water they need.

See Also

What Plants Need
Page 21

What Animals Need
Page 30

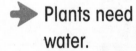

Plants need water.

People wash with water.

People drink water.

People use water for transportation. **Transportation** is the movement of people and things. Boats and ships move people and things on rivers, lakes, and oceans.

Water is also used in making electricity. People build dams on rivers. The flow of the river water turns machines that make electricity.

See Also

Oceans
Page 51

Water on Earth
Page 55

▲ People use water to help make electricity.

← People swim in water.

▲ People and things may travel by water.

Did You Know?
Each person in the U.S. uses about 80–100 gallons of water per day at home.

Caring for Resources

We depend on many natural resources. Some may be used up. So we have to use them carefully to make them last. Here are some tips.

Reduce

You care for natural resources when you **reduce**, or use less of a resource. Then there will be more for everyone in the future.

Reduce Your Use of	How?
water.	Take shorter showers.
electricity.	Turn off the lights when leaving.
paper.	Use both sides of a piece of paper.
gasoline.	Ride a bike, instead of using a car.

← Riding a bike instead of using a car reduces the use of gasoline.

Reuse

Another way to save resources is to reuse things. **Reuse** means to use again. You can use things that can be reused. You can also buy used items. This cuts down on trash. It saves money, too.

Do...	Instead of...
use drinking glasses you can wash again and again.	using paper cups that are thrown away.
use cloth grocery bags again and again.	using plastic bags that are thrown away.
look for a good bike at yard sales.	buying a new one right away.

Recycle

You can recycle to save resources. **Recycle** means to use the materials in old things to make new things. For example, old cans may be sorted, melted, and formed into new cans. Old newspapers may be made into new paper.

This symbol means that something can be recycled.

Physical Science

What is hard to push, but easy to pull?

Look at all the things around you. What are they like? How do they move and change? What makes them move and change?

How can you find out the answers to these questions? You can study physical science. **Physical science** is the study of matter, energy, motion, and forces.

Matter

Everything around you is matter. Air, juice, and cake are matter. You are matter, too.

Matter is anything that takes up space and has mass. **Mass** is the amount of matter in an object.

The cake, the juice, and the air in the balloons are matter.

Observing Properties

Matter has properties. A **property** is one part of what something is like. You can observe properties of matter with your senses.

See Also

Science Is Observing
Page 2

Rocks
Page 62

Properties You Can See

Color, shape, and size are some properties you can see.

These grapes are green, round, and small.

Properties You Can Feel

Texture and temperature are some properties you can feel.

This ice pop is smooth and cold.

Properties That Tell How Matter Acts

How matter acts is another way to think about its properties. Some objects sink. Others float. Some objects melt easily. Others do not.

⬆ The car and rocks sink. The ball floats.

⬆ Ice cream melts easily. The cone does not melt.

Sorting Matter

You can sort matter by its properties.
These blocks are sorted by size.

You could also sort these blocks by color or shape.

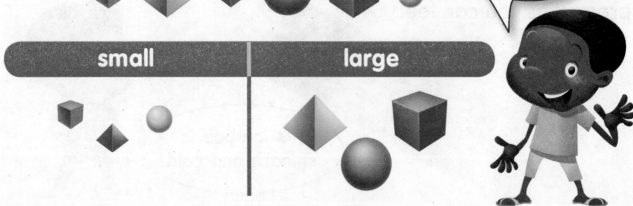

| small | large |

Forms of Matter

Matter has three forms. It can be a solid, a liquid, or a gas.

See Also

Units of Measure
Pages 121–123

Solids

A **solid** is matter that keeps its shape and volume. **Volume** is the amount of space that matter takes up.

Every solid has its own size and shape. It will not change in size or shape unless you do something such as cut, bend, or break it.

These objects will not change in size or shape.

Did You Know?
The solid form of water is ice.

Liquids

A **liquid** is matter that keeps its same volume, but does not have its own shape. It flows to take the shape of its container.

A liquid in a tall glass has the same shape as the glass. If the liquid is poured from the glass into a short cup, it will take the shape of the cup. A liquid does not change in volume unless you add more or take some away.

You can change a liquid's shape when you pour it into a different container.

Did You Know?
The water we drink is a liquid.

Gases

A **gas** is matter that does not have its own shape. It is the only kind of matter that fills all the space inside a container.

When you blow air into a balloon, the air spreads out inside. It fills the balloon. The air takes the shape of the balloon, too.

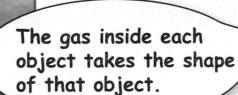

The gas inside each object takes the shape of that object.

Did You Know?
Water in the form of a gas that you cannot see is called **water vapor**.

Measuring Matter

You can use tools to measure some properties of matter.

Mass

You can use a balance to measure mass.

Look at this balance. The baseball has more mass than the tennis ball.

Size

You can use a ruler to measure how long or wide an object is.

See Also

Ruler, Measuring Cup
Pages 10–11

Units of Measure
Pages 121–123

Look at this ruler. The block is 2 inches wide.

Volume

You can use a measuring cup to measure volume.

Look at this measuring cup. The volume of the juice is 4 ounces.

Changing Matter

You can change matter in many ways. Some of these ways do not change matter into a different kind of matter.

Cutting and Folding

Cutting and folding can change matter. You can fold paper. You can cut it into pieces. The paper may be different shapes and sizes, but it is the same paper.

Cutting and folding do not change paper into a different kind of matter.

Mixing

When you put different kinds of matter together, you make a mixture. A **mixture** is something made of two or more things.

This salad is a mixture. You can separate the fruits. The apples, oranges, and bananas have not changed.

Some solids dissolve when you mix them with liquids. **Dissolve** means to mix with a liquid completely.

This drink mix dissolves in water. The mix is still there. You can taste it. It is just too small to see.

Water Can Change

Water may be solid, liquid, or gas. It can change form when heat is added or taken away.

Adding Heat

You can add heat to ice. The ice **melts**, or changes from solid to liquid water.

▲ The sun's heat melts this ice.

You can add heat to liquid water. The water **evaporates**, or changes to water vapor, a gas.

See Also

The Water Cycle
Pages 56–57

▲ The sun's heat changes this puddle into water vapor you cannot see.

Taking Away Heat

You can take away heat from water vapor. The water vapor **condenses**, or changes from a gas to liquid water.

⬆ Water vapor changes into water droplets on the window.

You can take away heat from liquid water. When you take away enough heat, the water **freezes**, or changes to solid ice.

Very cold temperatures changed this lake to ice.

Energy

Change happens all the time. Every change is caused by energy. **Energy** is something that can cause matter to move or change. There are many forms of energy.

Sound is energy you can hear.

Chemical energy is energy stored in food, fuel, and batteries.

Heat is energy that makes things warmer.

Electricity is energy from an electrical charge.

Light is energy that lets you see.

Kinetic energy is energy of movement.

Sound

Sound is energy you can hear. It is made when an object vibrates. To **vibrate** means to move back and forth very fast.

If you pluck a guitar string, you will hear a sound. You may see the string vibrate.

When the string stops vibrating, the sound stops.

Loudness

Sounds may be loud or soft. **Loudness** is how loud or soft a sound is.

← A tiger may make a loud sound.

→ A kitten may make a soft sound.

Pitch

Sounds may be high or low. **Pitch** is how high or low a sound is.

← A big dog has a bark with a low pitch.

↓ A small dog has a bark with a high pitch.

Did You Know?

Some singers can use pitch and loudness to shatter glass.

Light

Light is energy that lets you see. You can see objects that give off light.

The lamp, sun, and fire give off light.

You can also see objects when light shines on them. The amount of light can affect how you see objects.

Adding light can make objects look sharper and clearer. It can make colors look brighter.

Taking away light can make objects look fuzzy and unclear. It can make colors look dull and dark.

The amount of light changes the way we see things.

Motion and Forces

Motion is a change in position. A wagon is in motion when you move it along a sidewalk. You have to use a force to make the wagon move. A **force** is a push or a pull.

The girl pushes. She presses the wagon away.

The boy pulls. He tugs the wagon closer.

Pushes and Pulls

You can use a push or a pull to put something in motion. You can pull a door to open it. You can push the door to close it.

You can use a push or a pull to stop something from moving. When you catch a ball, you push it to stop its movement.

⬆ Catching a ball is a push.

You can use a push or a pull to change the direction of a moving object. When you kick a rolling ball, you are using a push. Your push makes it change direction.

⬆ Kicking a ball is a push.

How Things Move

Objects may move along different paths.

An object may move back and forth.

An object may move in a straight line.

An object may move round and round.

Measuring Motion

You can measure motion in several ways.

Distance

Distance is a measure of how far something moves. You compare where an object starts with where it stops. You can measure distance with a ruler, measuring tape, or yardstick.

Time

Time is a measure of how long it takes an object to go a distance. You compare when an object starts with when it stops. You can measure time with a clock or stopwatch.

See Also

Units of Measure
Pages 121–123

Speed

Speed is a measure of how fast an object is moving. There are three steps to find speed.

> Step 1: Find the distance the object goes.
>
> Step 2: Find how much time it takes the object to get there.
>
> Step 3: Compare the distance with the time.

A fast biker goes a distance in less time. A slow biker goes the same distance in more time.

Use distance and time to tell about speed. For example, 5 miles an hour may be your biking speed. So it takes 1 hour for you to go 5 miles

Some Kinds of Forces

Gravity, friction, and magnetism are kinds of forces. They act on objects without people pushing or pulling.

Gravity

Think about holding a ball. What happens if you let go? The ball falls to the ground. Gravity makes the ball move. **Gravity** is the force that pulls things toward the center of Earth. All objects fall to the ground unless another object holds them up.

A sled moves down a hill because of gravity. Gravity keeps us on the ground.

Friction

When an object moves on a surface, friction slows its movement. **Friction** is a force that holds back the movement of a sliding or rolling object.

A rough surface has more friction than a smooth one. Think about riding a bike. You have to push the pedals hard to move on a rough road. On a smooth road, you can ride more easily.

Magnetism

A **magnet** is an object that pulls on objects made of iron or steel. That pull between the magnet and the object is called **magnetism**.

A magnet does not attract all metals.

Magnets can be found in nature or made by people.

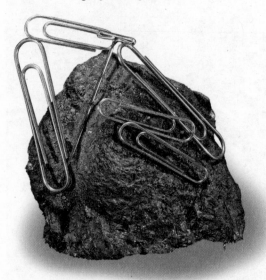

Lodestone is a magnet found in the ground.

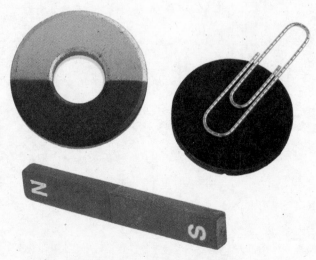

People make magnets that may be different shapes.

Magnets can pull on objects even if they are not touching. If a magnet is close enough, its pull can pass through air, water, and some solids.

People use magnets in many ways. Magnets hold cabinet doors closed. They are used in computers, telephones, televisions, electric motors, and many other things.

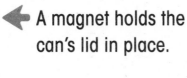 These magnets can hold papers or spell words.

This huge magnet is used to sort large metal scraps.

A magnet holds the can's lid in place.

This toy uses a magnet to move tiny bits of iron.

Almanac

This Almanac has helpful information that is important in science. The section about **Units of Measure** helps you understand how things are measured. The section on **Graphs and Time Lines** helps you understand how to read these visuals.

Units of Measure

Different countries use different units of measurement.

Metric Units

Most countries in the world use metric units.

Length and Distance

Unit: 1 millimeter (mm)		
10 millimeters	equals	1 centimeter (cm)
100 centimeters	equals	1 meter (m)
1000 meters	equals	1 kilometer (km)

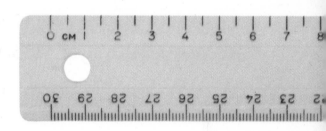

Volume

Unit: 1 milliliter (mL)		
1000 milliliters	equals	1 liter (L)

Temperature

Water freezes at 0 degrees Celsius (0°C).
Water boils at 100°C.

Customary Units

The United States uses customary units.

Length and Distance

Unit: 1 inch (in.)		
12 inches	equals	1 foot (ft)
3 feet	equals	1 yard (yd)
5280 feet	equals	1 mile (mi)

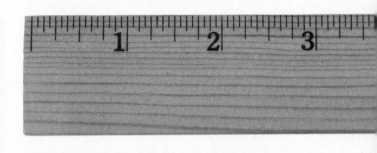

One yard is almost as long as 1 meter.

See Also

Using Science Tools
Pages 8–11

Temperature
Page 65

Solids
Page 95

Size, Volume
Page 99

Distance
Page 114

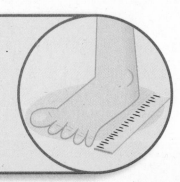

Did You Know?
The foot was first based on the length of a person's foot.

Volume

Unit: 1 teaspoon (tsp)		
3 teaspoons	equals	1 tablespoon (tbsp)
16 tablespoons or 8 fluid ounces (fl oz)	equals	1 cup (c)
2 cups	equals	1 pint (pt)
2 pints	equals	1 quart (qt)
4 quarts	equals	1 gallon (gal)

One quart has almost the same volume as 1 liter.

Temperature

Water freezes at 32 degrees Fahrenheit (32°F).

Water boils at 212°F.

Graphs and Time Lines

You can use graphs and time lines to organize and show information.

Picture Graph

A **picture graph** uses pictures to show information.

Leaves Found on October 2

maple	🍁	🍁	🍁	🍁	🍁	🍁
oak	🍂	🍂	🍂	🍂		
elm	🍃	🍃	🍃	🍃	🍃	

Tally Table

A **tally table** uses marks to show information.

Leaves Found on October 2		Total
maple	||||/	6
oak	////	4
elm	||||/	5

Each tally mark / stands for one leaf.

||||/ stands for five leaves.

Bar Graph

A **bar graph** uses bars to show information.

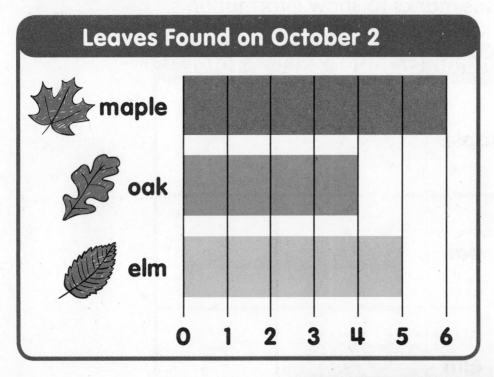

Leaves Found on October 2

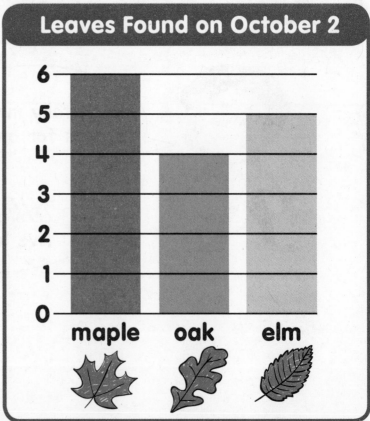

Leaves Found on October 2

These bar graphs show the same information.

Time Line

A time line shows when events took place. The numbers on a time line show the periods of time between events.

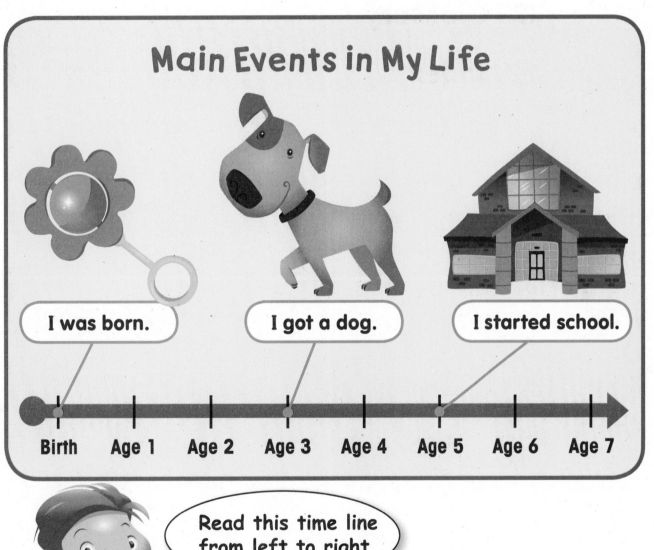

Main Events in My Life

I was born.   I got a dog.   I started school.

Birth   Age 1   Age 2   Age 3   Age 4   Age 5   Age 6   Age 7

Read this time line from left to right.

Yellow Pages

Glossary

amber: dried tree sap (page 39)

⬆ This insect was trapped in amber.

amphibian: an animal with smooth, moist skin (page 35)

⬆ A frog is a kind of amphibian.

animal: a living thing that cannot make its own food (page 29)

bar graph: a graph that uses bars to show information (page 126)

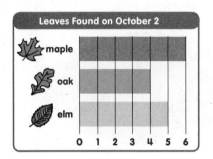

⬆ This is a bar graph.

bird: an animal that has feathers (page 33)

⬆ A turkey is a kind of bird.

canyon: a valley with steep sides (page 59)

⬆ Water formed this canyon.

chemical energy: energy stored in food, fuel, and batteries (page 104)

clay soil: soil that has very tiny rock bits (page 63)

▲ This is clay soil.

conclusion: an explanation of a pattern in data (page 7)

condense: to change from a gas to a liquid (pages 56, 103)

▲ Drops of water condensed on this window.

degree: the unit of measurement for temperature (page 9)

desert: an ecosystem that gets very little rain and a lot of sunlight (page 48)

▲ Deserts get little rain.

design process: a set of steps that engineers follow to solve problems (page 12)

dissolve: to completely mix with a liquid (page 101)

▲ Drink mix dissolves in water.

distance: a measure of how far something moves (page 114)

drought: a long time with very little rain (page 60)

⬆ This area is having a drought.

Earth science: the study of planet Earth and objects in the sky (page 52)

earthquake: a shaking of Earth's surface (page 61)

⬆ An earthquake made this road fall away.

ecosystem: all the living and nonliving things found in their environment (page 46)

⬆ This pond ecosystem has living and nonliving things.

electricity: energy from an electrical charge (page 105)

⬆ Electricity is a form of energy.

energy: something that can cause matter to move or change (page 104)

engineer: a person who solves problems by using math and science (page 12)

environment: all the living and nonliving things in a place (page 46)

erosion: when wind and water move rocks and soil (page 60)

⬆ Water caused erosion on this beach.

evaporate: to change from a liquid into a gas (pages 56, 102)

extinct: when no members of a kind of living thing are still alive (page 38)

fall: the season that follows summer (page 71)

fish: an animal that lives in water and breathes with gills (page 36)

⬆ Fish live in water.

flood: when streams, rivers, or lakes overflow onto land (page 61)

⬆ A flood may cause a lot of damage.

flower: a plant part that helps the plant reproduce by making fruits (page 26)

flower

⬆ This flower has made a fruit.

force: a push or a pull (page 110)

⬆ Kicking a ball shows a force.

forest: an ecosystem that gets enough rain and warmth for many trees to grow (page 47)

⬆ This is a forest.

fossil: what is left of an animal that lived long ago (page 38)

⬆ A fish left a fossil in the rock.

freeze: to change from liquid to solid (page 103)

⬆ This lake freezes in winter.

friction: a force that holds back the movement of a sliding or rolling object (page 117)

fruit: the plant part that holds seeds (page 26)

⬆ An apple is a fruit.

gas: matter that does not have its own shape and always fills all the space inside a container (page 97)

⬆ Gas fills the bubble.

germinate: to start to grow (page 27)

gills: body parts that take oxygen from water (page 31)

▲ A shark uses gills to breathe.

grassland: an ecosystem that is mostly dry (page 49)

▲ This is a grassland.

gravity: the force that pulls things toward the center of Earth (page 116)

▲ Gravity keeps a sled on the ground.

hail: pieces of ice that fall from clouds (page 67)

▲ Hail is white and cold.

hand lens: a tool that makes things look larger than they are (page 8)

▲ The girl holds a hand lens.

hearing: the sense that helps you learn how things sound (page 3)

▲ You use your ears for hearing.

heat: energy that makes things warmer (page 104)

⬆ Heat makes food hot.

hill: a high landform that is rounded and much smaller than a mountain (page 58)

⬆ These are hills.

hypothesis: an idea that tells what will happen and can be tested (page 5)

insect: an animal that has three body parts and six legs (page 37)

⬆ A bee is an insect.

investigation: a way to find out the answer to a question (page 4)

kinetic energy: energy of movement (page 105)

⬆ The bike has kinetic energy.

lake: a body of water with land all around it (page 55)

▲ The lake is blue.

landform: a natural land shape on Earth's surface (page 58)

▲ This landform is called an island.

larva: a stage in the life cycle of some insects; a caterpillar (page 45)

▲ A larva crawls on a leaf.

leaf: a plant part that uses sunlight, air, water, and nutrients to make food for the plant (page 25)

▲ This is a maple leaf.

life cycle: the changes a living thing goes through during its life (pages 27, 40)

light: energy that lets you see (page 105)

▲ The sun has light energy.

liquid: matter that keeps its same volume, but does not have its own shape (page 96)

⬆ A liquid takes the shape of its container.

living thing: something that needs food, water, and air to grow and change (page 18)

loam: soil that has a lot of plant and animal bits (page 63)

⬆ Loam has a lot of plant and animal bits.

loudness: how loud or soft a sound is (page 107)

lungs: body parts that take in air (page 32)

magnet: an object that pulls on objects made of iron or steel (page 118)

⬆ A magnet pulls on things made of steel or iron.

magnetism: the pull between a magnet and an object (page 118)

mammal: an animal that has hair or fur and feeds its young milk (page 32)

⬆ Dogs and cats are mammals.

mass: the amount of matter in an object (page 92)

matter: anything that takes up space and has mass (page 92)

measuring cup: a tool used to measure liquid amounts (page 11)

⬆ This is a measuring cup.

melt: to change from solid to liquid (page 102)

⬆ The sun's heat melts this ice.

mixture: something made of two or more things (page 101)

⬆ Fruit salad is a mixture.

moon: a huge ball of rock that orbits Earth (page 75)

⬆ The moon is in space.

motion: a change in position (page 110)

⬆ The wagon is in motion.

mountain: a landform that is much higher than the surrounding land (page 58)

⬆ This is a mountain.

natural resource: anything found in nature that people can use (page 80)

⬆ Water is a natural resource.

nonliving thing: anything that does not need food, water, and air (page 18)

nutrients: materials that help a plant grow (page 21)

⬆ Plants need nutrients from soil.

observe: to use the five senses to learn (page 2)

ocean: a large, deep body of salt water (pages 51, 55)

⬆ An ocean is large.

orbit: a planet's path (page 76)

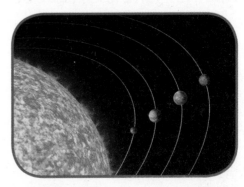

⬆ Each ring shows a planet's orbit.

physical science: the study of matter, forces, motion, and energy (page 91)

picture graph: a graph that uses pictures to show information (page 124)

pitch: how high or low a sound is (page 107)

⬆ A small dog usually has a bark with a high pitch.

plain: a flat land that spreads out over a long distance (page 59)

⬆ This is a plain.

planet: a large ball of rock or gas that moves around the sun (page 76)

⬆ Saturn is a planet.

plant: a living thing that uses sunlight to make food (page 20)

⬆ A sunflower is a plant.

plateau: a flat land that is higher than the land around it (page 59)

⬆ A plateau is flat.

precipitation: water that falls to Earth as rain, snow, sleet, or hail (pages 57, 66)

⬆ Snow is a kind of precipitation.

property: one part of what something is like (pages 62, 93)

⬆ A property of these grapes is that they are round.

pupa: the life stage of a butterfly or moth between a caterpillar and an adult (page 45)

⬆ This is a pupa.

rain: water that falls from clouds (pages 57, 66)

⬆ Rain falls from clouds.

rain forest: an ecosystem where rain falls almost every day (page 50)

⬆ A rain forest is green.

recycle: to use the materials in old things to make new things (page 89)

⬆ This symbol means something can be recycled.

reduce: to use less of a resource (page 88)

reproduce: to make new living things like oneself (page 18)

reptile: an animal with rough, dry skin covered with scales (page 34)

▲ An alligator is a reptile.

reuse: to use again (page 89)

river: a large body of flowing water (page 55)

▲ This is a river.

rock: a hard, nonliving object from the ground (page 62)

▲ Granite is a kind of rock.

roots: plant parts that take in water and nutrients from the soil (page 24)

▲ Plant roots usually grow in soil.

rotation: the spinning of a body in space (page 78)

▲ This shows Earth's rotation.

ruler: a tool used to measure how long something is (page 10)

▲ You can use a ruler to measure a leaf.

sandy soil: soil that has bits of rock you can see (page 63)

⬆ You can see bits of rock in sandy soil.

science: the study of the natural world (page 1)

scientist: a person who studies science (page 1)

season: a time of year that has a certain kind of weather (page 64)

seed: the part of a plant from which a new plant grows (page 26)

seed

⬆ An apple has seeds.

seedling: a young plant (page 28)

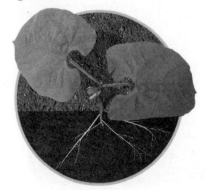

⬆ This is a bean seedling.

seed coat: the covering that protects a seed (page 27)

seed coat

⬆ A seed coat protects a seed.

sight: the sense that helps you learn how things look (page 3)

⬆ You use your eyes for sight.

sleet: small lumps of ice that form when rain falls through freezing air (pages 57, 67)

⬆ Sleet falls from the sky.

smell: the sense that helps you learn how things smell (page 3)

⬆ You use your nose to smell.

snow: solid water that falls from clouds (pages 57, 67)

⬆ Snow falls from clouds.

soil: the loose top layer of Earth's surface (page 63)

solar system: the sun and the planets around it (page 76)

⬆ This is a model of our solar system.

solid: matter that keeps its shape and volume (page 95)

⬆ This box is a solid.

sound: energy you can hear (page 104)

⬆ Music makes sound.

space: the area in all directions beyond Earth (page 73)

⬆ Stars are in space.

speed: a measure of how fast an object is moving (page 115)

spring: the season that follows winter (page 69)

star: a big ball of hot gases (page 75)

⬆ The sky has many stars.

stem: a plant part that moves water and nutrients up to the leaves (page 24)

⬆ Water moves up stems.

stream: a small body of flowing water (page 55)

⬆ This is a stream.

summer: the season that follows spring (page 70)

sun: the closest star to Earth (page 74)

⬆ The sun warms Earth.

tadpole: a young frog (page 43)

⬆ This is a tadpole.

tally table: a chart that uses marks to show information (page 125)

⬆ You use marks in a tally table.

taste: the sense that helps you learn which foods you like (page 3)

⬆ The girl tastes food.

temperature: a measure of how hot something is (page 65)

⬆ The temperature is 70 degrees.

test: a way to observe and measure what happens (page 5)

thermometer: a tool that is used to measure temperature (pages 9, 65)

⬆ A thermometer measures temperature.

time: a measure of how long it takes an object to go a distance (page 114)

time line: a kind of line that shows when events took place (page 127)

touch: the sense that helps you learn how things feel (page 3)

⬆ The boy touches the dog.

transportation: the movement of people and things (page 87)

⬆ Boats are transportation.

valley: the low land between mountains or hills (page 59)

⬆ The valley is green.

vibrate: to move back and forth very fast (page 106)

⬆ The strings vibrate.

volcano: a mountain with an opening in Earth (page 61)

⬆ This is a volcano.

volume: the amount of space matter takes up (pages 95)

water cycle: the movement of water between Earth and the air (page 56)

⬆ The model shows the water cycle.

water vapor: water in gas form (pages 56, 97)

weather: what the air is like outside (page 64)

weathering: when wind and water break down rock into small pieces (page 60)

wind: moving air (page 68)

⬆ The flags show how the wind is moving.

winter: the season that follows fall (page 72)

Index

Photo Credits

Key: (t) top   (b) bottom   (l) left
(r) right   (c) center   (bg) background

Front Cover
(b) ©Eric Isselee/Shutterstock
(tl) ©Michelle Bergkamp/Cutcaster
(l) ©Jim Craigmyle/Corbis
(r) ©Clover/Superstock
(c) ©StockTrek/Photodisc/Getty Images
(cr) ©DenisNata/Shutterstock
(bl) ©Brenda Anderson/Flickr/Getty Images

Back Cover
(tl) ©Renee Keith/E+/Getty Images
(cr) ©RF Company/Alamy Images
(br) ©Mark Thiessen/National Geographic Society/Corbis
(tr) ©DenisNata/Shutterstock
(bg) ©Brenda Anderson/Flickr/Getty Images

Table of Contents
iii (b) ©Robert Glusic/Corbis
iv (b) ©Jagodka/Shutterstock

Doing Science
2 (c) ©Corbis
3 (tl) ©Jupiter Images/Getty Images
(c) ©Digital Vision/Getty Images
(tr) ©Oliver Rossi/Corbis
(bl) ©SuperStock RF
(br) ©zhuda/Shutterstock
4 (br) ©Stockdisc/Getty Images
5 (cr) ©Stockbyte/Getty Images
(cr) ©Stockbyte/Getty Images
7 (br) ©Stockdisc/Getty Images
8 (b) ©Mitchell Funk/Photographer's Choice/Getty Images
9 (tl) ©Getty Images

Life Science
20 (bl) ©Mmphotos/Photolibrary/Getty Images
21 (tr) ©silvan/Flickr Open/Getty Images
(cr) ©Corbis
(br) ©Howard Rice/Getty Images
22 (bc) ©Brian Gadsby/Alamy Images
(br) ©Gabriela Insuratelu/Alamy
24 (bl) ©djgis/Shutterstock
(bc) ©Ron Evans/Garden Picture Library/Getty Images
(br) ©Genevieve Vallee/Alamy Images
25 (l) ©David Arky/Getty Images
(bc) ©Roine Magnusson/Getty Images
(br) ©George Diebold/Getty Images
(tc) ©George Diebold/Photographer's Choice RF/Getty Images
(tr) ©DAJ/amana images inc./Alamy Images
26 (cl) ©Francoise Sauze/Photo Researchers, Inc.
(cr) ©James P. Blair/Getty Images
(c) ©Stockbyte/Getty Images
(br) ©Corbis
27 (br) ©Biswaroop Mukherjee/National Geographic Society/Corbis
29 (r) ©Life on White/Alamy Images
(bc) ©Maria Gritsai/Alamy
(l) ©Getty Images
(tc) ©Kletr/Shutterstock

30 (c) ©Lushpix/Age Fotostock America, Inc.
(cr) ©Johan Swanepoel/Shutterstock
(br) ©Awei/Shutterstock
(tr) ©David Coleman/Alamy Images
31 (tr) ©Nagel Photography/Shutterstock
(cr) ©Nantawat Chotsuwan/Shutterstock
(bl) ©Tavnir Ibna Shafi/Flickr/Getty Images
(br) ©Ville Frisk/Shutterstock
32 (b) ©Jagodka/Shutterstock
(cl) ©Flickr/Ewen Charlton/Getty Images
(cr) ©Andy Sotiriou/Getty Images
33 (cl) ©Mircea Bezergheanu/Shutterstock
(cr) ©Joanne Harris and Daniel Bubnich/Shutterstock
(c) ©Mike Neale/Shutterstock
(br) ©Paul Souders/Corbis
34 (br) ©Kruglov Orda/Shutterstock
(cl) ©Tim Pleasant/Shutterstock
(bl) ©Comstock Images/Jupiterimages/Getty Images
35 (c) ©Comstock/Jupiterimages/Getty Images
(br) ©Yuri Maselov/Alamy Images
36 (bl) ©Kletr/Shutterstock
(br) ©Jeff Hunter/Photographer's Choice RF/Getty Images
(c) ©Alastair Pollock Photography/Flickr/Getty Images
37 (cl) ©Kuzmin Andrey/Shutterstock
(cr) ©Leighton Photography & Imaging/Shutterstock
(br) ©Eric Isselée/Shutterstock
(c) ©Christina Bollen/Alamy Images
38 (b) ©Gao Jianjun/Xinhua Press/Corbis
39 (r) ©Jonathan Blair/Corbis
(bl) ©Jason Edwards/National Geographic/Getty Images
(c) ©PjrStudio/Alamy Images

Earth Science
54 (c) NASA
55 (tr) ©PhotoDisc/Getty Images
(tcr) ©Frank Krahmer/Corbis
(bcr) ©Corbis
(br) ©Alamy Images
58 (cl) ©robert glusic/Corbis
(cr) ©Kevin Eaves/Shutterstock
(br) ©Frans Lemmens/Corbis
59 (tl) ©Jupiterimages/Getty Images
(tr) ©Katrina Brown/Fotolia
(bl) ©Glen Allison/Photodisc/Getty Images
(br) ©Herve Collart/Sygma/Corbis
60 (tr) ©Darren J. Bradley/Shutterstock
(cr) ©Roger Bamber/Alamy Images
(br) ©JP Laffont/Sygma/Corbis
61 (tr) ©Dennis M. Sabangan/epa/Corbis
(cr) ©Corbis
(br) ©Comstock/Getty Images
62 (bl) ©Tony Lilley/Alamy Images
(cl) ©vilax/Shutterstock
(br) ©Anthony Buckingham/Alamy Images
(bc) ©HMH
63 (cr) ©SPL/Photo Researchers, Inc.
(br) ©Sheila Terry/Photo Researchers, Inc.
64 (c) ©NataliSuns/Shutterstock
(l) ©Vibrant Image Studio/Shutterstock
(cr) ©mythja/Shutterstock
(r) ©cyberstock/Alamy Images
(cl) ©Solid Photo/Alamy Images
65 (bl) ©Chuck Haney/Danita Delimont Photography/NewsCom
(br) ©Chuck Haney/Danita Delimont/NewsCom

66 (c) ©Jim Corwin/Alamy Images
   (br) ©Goodshoot/Jupiterimages/Getty Images
67 (tr) ©leonid_tit/Shutterstock
   (cr) ©Peter Essick/Aurora/Getty Images
   (bcr) ©Limor Sidi/Alamy Images
   (br) ©Giovanni Mereghetti/Marka/Alamy Images
69 (b) ©Getty Royalty Free
   (tr) ©Willy Matheisl/Picture Press/Getty Images
70 (c) ©Jupiterimages/Getty Images
   (tr) ©Willy Matheisl/Picture Press/Getty Images
71 (c) ©Hill Creek Pictures/UpperCut Images/Getty Images
   (tr) ©Willy Matheisl/Picture Press/Getty Images
72 (tr) ©Willy Matheisl/Picture Press/Getty Images
   (c) ©elina/Shutterstock
73 (c) ©Media Union/Shutterstock
74 (cr) SOHO (ESA & NASA)
   (cl) ©Brand X Pictures/Getty Images
75 (cl) NASA/Hubble Heritage Team
   (cr) NASA
   (br) ©Photodisc/Getty Images
   (br) ©Photodisc/Getty Images
   (br) ©Photodisc/Getty Images
78 (b) ©Kord.com/age fotostock
79 (b) ©Kord.com/age fotostock
81 (cl) ©Siede Preis/PhotoDisc/Getty Images
   (cr) ©Thinkstock/Comstock Images/Getty Images
   (bl) ©Artville/Getty Images
82 (cl) ©Le Do/Shutterstock
   (cr) ©inxti/Shutterstock
   (bl) ©Kochneva Tetyana/Shutterstock
   (bc) ©Tommaso Guicciardini/Photo Researchers, Inc.
   (br) ©Getty Images RF
83 (tc) ©Siede Preis/Photodisc/Getty Images
   (bl) ©Artville/Getty Images
   (bc) ©Yuri Samsonov/Shutterstock
84 (bl) ©Zelenskaya/Shutterstock
   (br) ©Ryan McVay/Photodisc/Getty Images
86 (bl) ©Getty Images
   (c) ©Corbis Premium RF/Alamy Images
   (r) ©Photodisc Collection/Getty Images
87 (br) ©Getty Images/PhotoDisc/Don Farrall
   (cr) ©Auscape/Universal Images Group/Getty Images
   (cl) ©Andy/Fotolia
   (c) ©Allsop/Shutterstock

Physical Science
93 (b) ©Stockbyte/Getty Images
94 (tr) ©Digital Image copyright ©2004 PhotoDisc
95 (br) ©Royalty-Free/Corbis
96 (br) ©Getty Images
97 (cl) ©Stockdisc/Getty Images
   (cl) ©Stock shots by itani/Alamy Images
   (cr) ©Royalty-Free/Corbis
   (br) ©Eiichi Onodera/Getty Images
102 (cr) ©Shutterstock
103 (tr) ©Vladimir Godnik/Getty Images
   (bl) ©JLImages/Alamy Images
   (br) ©Andrew Bain/Lonely Planet Images/Getty Images
107 (tl) ©Dave King/Dorling Kindersley/Getty Images
   (tr) ©Tony Campbell/Shutterstock
   (cr) ©dogboxstudio/Shutterstock
   (c) ©Erik Lam/Shutterstock
   (br) ©Steve Bronstein/Stone/Getty Images
108 (cr) ©The Photolibrary Wales/Alamy Images
   (b) ©solo deo gloria/Flickr/Getty Images
109 (cl) ©Ron Watts/First Light/Getty Images
   (cr) ©Ron Watts/First Light/Getty Images
118 (bl) ©Joel Arem/Photo Researchers/Getty Images
119 (cr) ©Photolibrary

Yellow Pages
129 (cr) ©Mike Neale/Shutterstock
   (cl) ©Comstock/Jupiterimages/Getty Images
   (tl) ©PjrStudio/Alamy Images
   (br) ©Katrina Brown/Fotolia
130 (bl) ©Vladimir Godnik/Getty Images
131 (tr) ©JP Laffont/Sygma/Corbis
   (cl) ©Dennis M. Sabangan/epa/Corbis
132 (tl) ©Roger Bamber/Alamy Images
   (cr) ©Comstock/Getty Images
   (br) ©Francoise Sauze/Photo Researchers, Inc.
   (tr) ©Kletr/Shutterstock
   (bl) ©Willy Matheisl/Picture Press/Getty Images
133 (cr) ©James P. Blair/Getty Images
   (bl) ©Jason Edwards/National Geographic/Getty Images
   (tr) ©Andrew Bain/Lonely Planet Images/Getty Images
134 (tl) ©Stock shots by itani/Alamy Images
   (cl) ©Nantawat Chotsuwan/Shutterstock
   (br) ©Limor Sidi/Alamy Images
135 (cr) ©Kuzmin Andrey/Shutterstock
   (tr) ©Kevin Eaves/Shutterstock
   (cl) ©Digital Vision/Getty Images
136 (cr) ©George Diebold/Getty Images
   (cl) ©Alamy Images
   (bl) ©Frans Lemmens/Corbis
137 (tr) ©SPL/Photo Researchers, Inc.
   (tl) ©The Photolibrary Wales/Alamy Images
138 (tl) ©Jagodka/Shutterstock
   (br) ©Photodisc/Getty Images
   (tr) ©Shutterstock
139 (cr) ©Howard Rice/Getty Images
   (br) ©Photodisc/Getty Images
   (cl) ©robert glusic/Corbis
140 (tr) ©Glen Allison/Photodisc/Getty Images
   (br) ©silvan/Flickr Open/Getty Images
   (bl) ©dogboxstudio/Shutterstock
141 (tl) ©Herve Collart/Sygma/Corbis
   (cr) ©Jim Corwin/Alamy Images
   (cl) ©leonid_tit/Shutterstock
142 (bl) ©Tim Pleasant/Shutterstock
   (tr) ©Corbis
   (cr) ©vilax/Shutterstock
143 (cr) ©Stockbyte/Getty Images
   (bl) ©Sheila Terry/Photo Researchers, Inc.
144 (bl) ©Peter Essick/Aurora/Getty Images
   (cl) ©JUPITER IMAGES/Getty Images
   (tr) ©zhuda/Shutterstock
   (cr) ©leonid_tit/Shutterstock
145 (tr) ©Willy Matheisl/Picture Press/Getty Images
   (bl) ©Media Union/Shutterstock
   (br) NASA/Hubble Heritage Team
146 (tl) ©djgis/Shutterstock
   (cl) ©Frank Krahmer/Corbis
   (tr) ©Brand X Pictures/Getty Images
   (bl) ©Willy Matheisl/Picture Press/Getty Images
147 (bl) ©Chuck Haney/Danita Delimont Photography/
        NewsCom
   (br) ©Oliver Rossi/Corbis
   (tl) ©SuperStock RF
148 (cl) ©Jupiterimages/Getty Images
   (tr) ©Corbis
   (tl) ©Auscape/Universal Images Group/Getty Images
149 (cl) ©Willy Matheisl/Picture Press/Getty Images